THE

GHOSTLY TALES

OF

NEW
ORLEANS

Published by Arcadia Children's Books
A Division of Arcadia Publishing
Charleston, SC
www.arcadiapublishing.com

Copyright © 2021 by Arcadia Children's Books
All rights reserved

Spooky America is a trademark of Arcadia Publishing, Inc.

First Published in 2021

Manufactured in the United States

ISBN 978-1-4671-9818-9

Library of Congress Control Number: 2021932674

Spooky America

THE
GHOSTLY TALES
OF
NEW
ORLEANS

LAURA ROACH DRAGON

Adapted from *Haunted New Orleans* by Troy Taylor

arcadia
CHILDREN'S BOOKS

MI
AL
GA

LOUISIANA

TX

FL

GULF OF MEXICO

NEW ORLEANS

Table of Contents & Map Key

Introduction 3

🏛 Chapter 1. Cities of the Dead 15

Chapter 2. Dark Places and Terrible Deeds. 29

    1 Ghouls of Fourth Street

    2 Beautiful Children of Saratoga Street

    3 Cherokee Street

    4 Former Sausage Factory

    5 Saint Peter Street

🏛 Chapter 3. The Voodoo Queen of New Orleans 51

🏛 Chapter 4. Prove Your Love 65

🏛 Chapter 5. The Phantom Army 75

🏛 Chapter 6. Locked Up. 81

Chapter 7. Tourist Trappers .95

    6 Andrew Jackson Hotel

    7 Hotel Provincial

    8 Bourbon Orleans Hotel

    9 Former site of O'Flaherty's

    10 Commander's Palace

    11 Old Absinthe House

French Quarter, New Orleans

Introduction

New Orleans is a beautiful old city in Louisiana situated on the Mississippi River. It's famous for its colorful Mardi Gras celebrations and the famous French Quarter—a district in New Orleans that is filled with landmarks and attractions that are a year-round delight for tourists and locals alike.

New Orleans was founded in 1718 by the governor of French Louisiana, Jean Baptiste

Le Moyne de Bienville. Bienville was born in Canada, and his desire for fortune in the New World was, to him, a quest to find the promised land. But what he found when he arrived was anything but land with promise.

The soil was soaked with water from the mighty river that flooded the area every year. This presented the most undesirable conditions. Plus, it was hot. *Really* hot. And really humid. Bienville and his people were not entirely prepared for the heat pressing in from all sides, nor for sloshing through swamp water and getting swarmed by mosquitoes.

Surely they prayed that they'd never trip over a hungry alligator lurking below the surface, waiting to feed. That hidden horror in the gloomy water must have chilled the blood of every man,

4

woman, and child in Bienville's camp (despite the miserable heat). But in spite of all this, Bienville was persistent in his search, and finally, he found a natural high spot of dry land along the Mississippi River. It was here, Bienville was convinced, that he could start developing his city. But there was one small problem.

The settlers in his camp were *not* impressed with his choice of land. One account described the location as being just two thin strips of land locked in by treacherous marshland.

Bienville understood their frustration. He decided they would have to drain the marsh. He knew it was the only way the settlement could expand and become a suitable place for families and businesses. But he also had other reasons to drain the marsh: the settlers would not be happy if their homes sank into the mud, to say nothing of the fact that the excess water would make farming all but impossible. It turned out to be a smart decision by Bienville.

Farmers selected crops like cotton, corn, and sweet potatoes, which they knew would grow well in highly saturated soil. Rice farming was also introduced, and sugarcane was discovered already growing in the area. It became a valuable commodity for both cooking and trade.

New Orleans is also known for its levees. Levees are embankments that form naturally (or are built) along bodies of water to keep water on one side and dry land on the other. Some natural levees existed when Bienville and his people arrived. Then they built more to keep the waters from flooding into their new city. As a result, the land began to dry. This made travel to New Orleans more accessible, as more settlers were making their way to the city, which was shaping up to be more like the promised land that Bienville first dreamed about.

Nonetheless, the city of New Orleans was not without its challenges. Death was a constant possibility, as either floods or alligators or insect-borne disease could strike at any time. France had been supporting the settlers by shipping food and supplies to the colony. But France was in the middle of fighting with Britain at the time, and the conflict was gutting France financially. Without aid from France, the future of the colony was in doubt. Not long after, the French government abandoned the colony, recalling Bienville from his duties in New Orleans and leaving the colonists to fend for themselves

The men and women of the colony were intent on staying in New Orleans, regardless

of who was in charge. New Orleans was their home now, and they had no plans to leave. But throughout the late 1700s, control over New Orleans changed frequently between France and Spain. Many of the French-born colonists were furious about being under Spanish rule. The Spanish government would send "governors" to New Orleans to keep an eye on the colonists, many of whom were threatened with slavery. Between the Spanish forces and the colonists' rebel uprising, blood soaked the ground in one conflict after another in New Orleans. To avoid peril within the city, many colonists spread out to the neighboring bayou regions, bringing their culture, recipes, and way of life to other parts of Louisiana.

In 1800, the colonists were happy to discover that Spain had given New Orleans back to France. But France was at war again, under Napoleon this time, and yellow fever had stricken New Orleans, so Spain was asked to continue managing the city. Meanwhile, the newly formed United States government had noticed the city's busy port and the huge river that could open up the entire country to trade. The Mississippi River flowed past Kentucky, as well as nine other states within the American territory. This made exports of rice and cotton up the river into the American territories very easy and created a trade route that brought textile, furniture, and more back to New Orleans.

In 1803, a cash-strapped France agreed to sell New Orleans and the whole Louisiana Territory to Thomas Jefferson—the famous Louisiana Purchase. The sale doubled the size of the rapidly expanding United States. In 1812, Louisiana became the 18th state in the American Union. France was paid just four cents an acre. Can you imagine what an acre of land in New Orleans would cost today? A lot more than four cents, that's for sure!

In the early 1900s, yellow fever ran rampant throughout New Orleans. A water purification plant was built, which helped relieve the city from most of the mosquito swarms they'd endured, and as a result, infections became less frequent. In addition, a spillway was built, which further protected the city from the encroaching waters of the Mississippi River.

The New Orleans of today is wonderfully diverse and full of music, food, and happy people. The Mardi Gras parades hosted by the city include giant floats that roll through the streets, showering people with beads and prizes. There are cool refreshing lakes and bayous where families enjoy sun-filled days of fishing or boating. But there's another side to this richly complex city—an ugly, frightening side. Remember, New Orleans is very old and has countless dark secrets. Like all cities, there's a history of shameful and wicked events—events that people don't like to talk about.

Strange happenings, scary people, and many many ghosts call New Orleans home. So, grab a flashlight and follow me into the darkness, friends. You're about to read the spine-tingling ghost stories that New Orleans has to offer.

Metairie Cemetery, New Orleans

Cities of the Dead

New Orleans has a way of sending off their dearly departed that is different from anywhere else in the country. A long time ago, a New Orleans family gathered at the edge of a newly dug grave. They had worked hard to make a life in New Orleans, and now they had lost a member of their clan. Their loved one was lying silent in the rough-made wooden coffin. Sniffles could be heard in the small crowd that managed to make it to the service. Tears dripped down cheeks, disappearing into the mounded dirt waiting to be shoveled back into the grave.

One family member walked up to the gravesite and noticed something puzzling. There was water in the grave. She turned to the clergyman presiding over the ceremony. He shrugged, saying there was nothing that could be done. That was just how New Orleans was: any hole dug farther down than a few feet would fill up with water. Remember, the city is very close to sea level and surrounded by rivers, lakes, and marshes.

The family allowed the service to go on. The cemetery custodian lowered the coffin into the grave. But the coffin just bobbed and rocked on the water that filled most of grave. Those gathered waited in suspense. Surely, they thought, the box will fill up with water and sink, but the coffin continued to float.

The custodian put his foot on the coffin and pushed down, holding the box under the water. When he lifted his foot, the coffin bobbed back up again. The custodian then tried shoveling dirt onto the top of the coffin. The box rocked, causing the dirt to slide off into the water. He continued to throw dirt on the wobbling box, but it just slid into the water.

Then the mourners had a try. They scattered from the site, gathering stones and placing them on top of the coffin. The rickety box

tilted under the rocks and then broke apart, leaving their loved one floating atop the water with the broken pieces of wood.

A new coffin was fetched, and their loved was placed into it. Everyone filled the hole with dirt before the new coffin was laid inside. There was just enough room to lay the coffin on top of the muddy slurry and cover it with the last of the dirt. The family sighed in relief and went home.

A week later, a storm came through with lots and lots of rain. When the family next visited their loved one's grave, they were horrified to see that the rainstorm had soaked the ground,

and the coffin had again been pushed to the surface.

It was clear to everyone that they had to find a different way to bury people. The city decided that the best way would be to bury their dead above ground. They began building tombs, small structures where whole families could be laid to rest together. At first, the tombs were basic four-walled structures. But once people got used to this way of housing the dead, they began creating fancier tombs, decorating them with statues of angels and vases for flowers, especially the rich folk of the city. But rich or poor, fancy or plain, all of the tombs were gathered together in the graveyard. After a while, people began to notice how much the graveyard appeared like a small town. The citizens began to call it a "City of the Dead." The nickname stuck, and New Orleans cemeteries are still called that to this day.

One of the best-known cities of the dead is St. Louis Cemetery No. 1. It is said that in the 1930s, cab drivers avoided St. Louis Cemetery No. 1. When asked why, they would tell a story about a driver who once picked up a girl in a white dress and took her to the address she said was her home. When they arrived, she asked him to tell the man in the house to come out and meet her at the car. The cab driver went to the door and did as the girl asked. The man who answered the door asked the driver what the girl looked like. The driver told him. The man in the house became very sad. He told the cab driver that the girl was his wife who died years ago. She had been laid to rest in a lovely white dress—her wedding dress, in fact.

The man then told the driver that he wasn't the first cabbie this happened to. The cab driver hurried to his car and looked inside for the girl. She was nowhere to be found.

The cabbie collapsed on the ground in fear. After hearing his story, his fellow cab drivers agreed they never wanted to drive past that cemetery again.

Over time, St. Louis Cemetery No. 1 became overcrowded, so the Metairie Cemetery was built. Ponds, tree-shaded paths, and beautiful flower beds make it feel more like a park than a city of the dead. In fact, it has been named one of the most beautiful cemeteries in the country. From the beginning, the richest and most powerful people chose the Metairie Cemetery over any of the others. And of course, the Metairie Cemetery is a resting place known for ghostly activity.

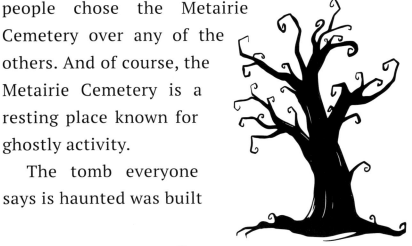

The tomb everyone says is haunted was built

St. Louis Cemetery No. 1

on a small hill. It belonged to a business woman named Josie Arlington, who had become very rich in New Orleans. She had worked her way up from nothing and was very proud of her success. The rich and powerful people of New Orleans, however, refused to speak to her or invite her to their parties because she had been born into a poor family. They felt she was not good enough to be in their society.

Josie wanted to teach them a lesson. She decided they couldn't stop her from being "in their society" after death. She planned to build the most beautiful tomb in the most beautiful cemetery in the city. So she went to the Metairie Cemetery, bought land on the little hill, and then hired a specialist to design a fabulous tomb. The rich and powerful folks complained, but they couldn't stop her.

When the specialist completed the building,

people from far away came, interested to see the beautiful tomb the rich people were complaining about. They saw a tomb made of red marble with stone pillars of fire at each side. On the staircase leading to the tomb's entrance was a bronze statue of a woman climbing the stairs, a bouquet of roses in the crook of one arm and the other reaching to open the door.

Some people went to see the tomb at night. They returned with a story that made the tomb even more famous. They said that as they gazed upon the tomb, it seemed to burst into flames. The red marble appeared covered with fire that licked out from the stone.

After that, the cemetery was jammed every night with sightseers. This upset the rich and powerful even more, as their exclusive cemetery was overrun. Josie died several years later and was placed inside her "flaming tomb." After Josie's funeral, rumors started. People said they'd seen the statue on the steps move. Two cemetery attendants reported that they saw the statue wandering around the park. They tried to follow, but it vanished right before their eyes. There are records saying that the statue was found in other areas of the cemetery and had to be carried back to the tomb.

Josie had a whole year in her tomb before her family moved her out and sold the famous

burial chamber to another family. The tomb went for a high price. Josie's family refused to tell anyone where they had placed her, saying they didn't want the crowds following her to her new crypt. The statue at the Metairie crypt never walked again, but there are stories of someone entering the cemetery and pounding on the door of the tomb. People say it is Josie, wanting to be back in her hard-won resting place.

Dark Places and Terrible Deeds

All cities have their secrets. Let's take a look at some of the dark places around New Orleans and the terrible deeds that happened there.

THE GHASTLY GHOULS OF FOURTH STREET

There once was a house on Fourth Street that people said was SO haunted, no one lived there longer than a couple of weeks. In fact, some people ran away after only *one day*. The owner was very unhappy about this. Not only was it impossible to rent the house (which he needed to do to earn money), but he was also worried the house would get vandalized if it sat empty. He finally offered the house to some people

who couldn't afford a place of their own. All he asked was that they keep the house clean and safe from thieves.

The new tenants tried, but after only one horrible night, they fled to a smaller building behind the house. They told neighbors that the lights in the house turned on and off by themselves, there were strange knocking sounds, and at times they could see ghostly faces appearing in the windows. But the most frightening thing was when the kitchen door opened by itself, and in the bright moonlight, they saw hazy-looking spirits crawl around the kitchen on their hands and knees.

So the tenants settled into the outbuilding, and the landlord went back to looking for people to live in the actual house. At long last, he found two elderly women who agreed to give it a try. They stayed a whole week before they grabbed their belongings and ran for the door. They, too, saw the crawling ghosts, but the two ladies said the ghosts did more in the kitchen than just crawl. First of all, they were covered with blood. Throughout the week, they broke dishes, tore up clothing, and smeared dirt and food on the sofa. The final horror occurred when one of the creatures pulled off his leg and *threw it at them*. The ladies said they couldn't take it anymore and moved out.

The landlord realized he had to make a change. He decided to tear up the floor in the house and replace it with a new one. What do you think the workmen found beneath the floor? SKELETONS. Did the landlord know they were there? He never did say. He had the skeletons taken away and laid to rest in a cemetery. The spirts went away. After that, no one ever saw any spirits in the house again.

Beautiful Children

In another part of New Orleans, on Saratoga Street, people talked of a house that was haunted by a man who loved gold more than he loved family. In life, he was a hardworking person who spent little and saved a lot. He would sit in the light of his lamp, rubbing his fingers over his golden coins. He called his money "my beautiful children" and petted and polished each bit of gold, stacking the coins one on top of another and counting them over and over again.

One night, he crept into the backyard and buried the coins in the yard. No one knows why he did this, but he was always worrying that someone would sneak in and steal his "beautiful children." The old man passed away soon after, without telling anyone where he had buried the fortune.

Soon after the funeral, the spirit of the gold-obsessed man left his tomb and revisited his yard to search for his coins. He apparently couldn't find them because he continued to appear in the yard for several years. He would beg for his "beautiful children" to tell him where he had hidden them. Neighbors would watch when he appeared, hoping to find out where the treasure was buried. But the old man seemed never to find it.

Word got out of the lost fortune, and others came to search. Over time, every inch of the yard was dug up, but the gold was never found.

THE NEVER-ENDING FEUD

Ollie Voss loved living on Cherokee Street in New Orleans, with one exception: mean Mr. Abner White, who lived just a few doors down from her. Ollie was not alone. All of the neighbors living in the 200 block of Cherokee Street were afraid of the hateful old man. But Ollie and her friends disliked him the most.

Abner loved to pick on kids, calling them ugly names and always accusing them of things they didn't do. But Ollie knew that Mr. White kept his meanest names and words for her. Avoiding him became a way of life.

One day, despite her sharp-eyed attempts to never cross his path, he appeared from nowhere. He accused her of something she hadn't done and grabbed her, shaking her violently. After that, Ollie decided she'd had enough. She stopped avoiding him and began showering insults on him anytime she spotted him outside of his home. He, of course, showered his abuse right back. The war continued until one morning, Abner White didn't wake up ever again.

The neighbors all down the block expressed their relief at his passing, but their cheers turned to tears when, a few days later, a freak accident at home killed poor little Ollie. The mean old man and the brave girl who opposed him were entombed in the same cemetery. And in an unhappy twist, right next to one another.

A short time later, the houses on Cherokee Street were suddenly pelted with bricks. The attack ended in the blink of an eye, but the startled occupants burst from their homes, angrily searching for the offender.

But no one was found.

They all gathered together, grumbling and arguing about who would throw bricks at them. The next evening, it happened again.

And the next. And the next. The neighborhood watched carefully, but no one could figure out where the bricks were coming from or why their houses were being targeted. The police searched everywhere and found nothing.

Finally, one of the families came up with a possible answer. Perhaps it was Ollie Voss and Abner White still fighting it out in the afterlife. They sighed and endured daily brick showers for quite a while. But then, one day, the bricks stopped falling. They never fell again. The relieved neighbors wondered who won the battle: Abner or Ollie. Each and every neighbor chose little Ollie.

REVENGE IN THE SAUSAGE SHOP

Hans Muller and his wife moved to New Orleans from Germany and opened a sausage factory over on Ursulines Street. They worked hard together, and the factory did very well. As more and more money rolled in, greedy Hans Muller decided to get rid of his wife so he could have everything all to himself. Divorce wasn't really an option at that time, not if he wanted to keep his customers. So Hans decided to get rid of his wife for good. Yes. I mean *murder*.

After Mr. Muller killed his wife, he needed to get rid of the evidence. What do you think he did? Yup, he ground up the, er, evidence by putting her body through the sausage grinder. Really.

The neighbors noticed Han's wife had disappeared. When they asked where she was, he told them that she had returned to Germany.

Sometime later, while working in the factory alone, Mr. Muller heard a loud thumping sound from giant boiler. He hurried over to to find what was causing the noise. And that's when the horrifying, blood-covered ghost of his dead

wife burst from the shadows. One look at her mangled head and her blood-soaked hands reaching for his throat sent him shrieking out of the factory. He screamed so loud that the neighbors came running out of their houses. They asked what was going on, and he told them he'd fallen asleep and had a nightmare.

After that, Mr. Muller had a hard time. He often cowered in the back of the butcher shop. Then a customer took some sausage home and began frying it up for lunch. Suddenly she noticed something strange in the meat—a golden wedding ring!

She called the police. They went to find Mr. Muller to ask

about the ring in the sausage. They found him at the factory, curled up in a corner, screaming and crying that his wife was going to come out of the sausage grinder and kill him.

The police brought him to an insane asylum, which is where Hans Muller lived out the rest of his life, screaming in terror about the ghost of his wife.

The sausage factory was sold, but Mrs. Muller's ghost didn't leave. She continued to appear in the factory, terrifying the employees. The new owner would hire workers only to see them quit right away. No one wanted to be in the shop after dark. Then, one day, the ghost didn't show up to terrorize the work crew. The new owner learned that Hans Muller had died in the asylum that day.

Everyone assumed that Hans Muller's wife had gotten her revenge after all.

THE EVIL DENTIST

On St. Peter Street, there was an apartment no one wanted to live in. A pair of ghosts was the reason why. Lots of people tried to live in the apartment, but they always left after seeing the ghosts act out a horrible death scene over and over.

It seems that way back in the 1850s, there was a dentist named Deschamps who believed he had supernatural powers. He decided to experiment with these powers and talked a young woman into allowing him to hypnotize her. He was certain that once he had her in a hypnotic state, she would be able to talk to the dead and find out their secrets and hidden treasures. But no matter how hard he tried, his efforts never produced any information. He grew angry. He blamed the young woman for his failure, and then he killed her.

Deschamps was arrested, tried for murder, and found guilty. He was executed for his crime.

Then the appearances began. In the years that followed, the ghost of the dentist and the young woman returned to the scene of the crime and replayed the young woman's murder. Most said that they never saw either ghost by themselves, only with each other.

One young man who attempted to live in the apartment was taking a bath when the

angry ghost of Dr. Deschamps surprised him in the bathroom. The frightened man scrambled out of the tub and ran naked into the street! A policeman chased after him, shouting for him to stop and waving a coat for him to wear. The man stopped running and gratefully covered himself up. But he absolutely refused to go back to the apartment. His friends were called, and they offered to pick up his belongings when they realized how frightened he was.

Eventually, the apartment was sold and became a restaurant. The employees who worked there were *also* haunted by the murderer and his victim. But this time, the ghosts moved objects. Dishes, skillets, and cooking pans were there one moment and gone the next. The staff would then find their missing kitchen tools in a completely different part of the building. Strange and annoying indeed.

In the Rose Garden

There is an ages-old New Orleans legend of a palatial mansion where a fabulously rich father and his gorgeous daughter resided. The pair dominated the social scene of old New Orleans for decades thanks to his money and her beauty. But as happens, the father eventually died, and his daughter's unblemished beauty faded away, and nothing was heard of them for years.

One day, a newspaper editor stumbled across an old picture of the daughter. He did some research and discovered she was still alive. Since she had to be more than a hundred years old by then, the editor felt an article investigating her current life would make an excellent feature, and so he dispatched a young news reporter to get the story.

The reporter arrived expecting a stunningly beautiful house. The house was stunning, but it was no longer beautiful. Nature had run wild, strangling the old building. Thick vines crept up crumbling walls and algae-stained masonry. Filthy windows displayed torn, sagging curtains, and patches of flaking paint left dark spots everywhere. A servant met the reporter at the door and led him upstairs to a room where the elderly woman awaited him.

The woman was extremely old. Most of her hair was gone, her skin was paper-thin, and there were gaps in her mouth where her teeth should have been. In honor of his visit, she had decked herself out with lavish rings and necklaces of diamonds and pearls and a tiara with jewels that flashed in the dim light of the room.

The old woman began to tell her story and the reporter noticed she still saw herself as a young woman. She even mentioned her father being away from home when the reporter knew that her father had been dead for decades. But he continued to write down what she said.

Most of her story centered around the many men who loved her and wanted to marry her. She spoke of how her beauty drew in handsome men who refused to leave the mansion after meeting her.

She went on, claiming these men would do anything for her. They were constantly trying to win her affection. She touched her jewels and told him that the men had brought them for her to wear. She described the enormous rose garden in the back of the house where she would meet and walk with the men who sought her hand in marriage.

Finally, the old lady's eyelids began to sag, and before long, she was snoring away in her chair. Having heard so much about how grand the house used to be, the reporter slipped away and began to explore the other rooms. He hadn't gone far before a ghost, dressed in filthy, old-fashioned clothing, appeared before him, blocking his way. The ghost said nothing but waved for the reporter to follow him. Frightened, but curious, the reporter followed the phantom to a room at the end of the hall. The reporter opened the door and saw a huge mob of young male ghosts. Who were they? What were they doing there? Fearing for his life, the reporter slammed the door, stumbled down the stairs, and ran out of the house. He never returned.

A year later, the old lady passed away, and new owners began repairing the neglected mansion. Workmen outside tore down a wall in the rose garden. Beneath it, they were shocked and horrified to find skeletons. Lots and lots of skeletons. There were about fifty of them, all jumbled together. When the young reporter saw the news report detailing the mass grave, he realized who those ghosts he'd encountered in that terrifying room had been. They were the tragic spirits of the suitors the daughter and her father did away with.

The elderly lady might have been wrong about her age and her father being alive, but she knew what she was talking about when she said the men who came to meet her never left the rose garden again.

The Voodoo Queen of New Orleans

Voodoo is a religion that originated in West Africa. It gave heart, strength, and power to enslaved people for decades and is a huge part of New Orleans's past.

Voodoo was founded in Africa and spread to Haiti when Africans were kidnapped from their homes, brought to the island, and forced into slavery. The white men who took them were cruel and harsh, so the African people embraced their religion to help them through the horrors of being enslaved. It was also a way of getting back at the slave masters. The French kidnappers did not understand voodoo and were afraid of it.

Masters demanded that the African people give up their religion, threatening to harm them if they did not. But the people continued their rituals and eventually managed to drive the masters out of Haiti. Unfortunately, when the white masters left, they took many African slaves with them.

The masters and their captives sailed to the only city in America that spoke French: New Orleans. And at once, Voodoo began to spread in the city.

As in Haiti, the belief in Voodoo and the power of the Voodoo priests helped the African people in New Orleans. And again, the slave owners wanted to stamp Voodoo out.

Into this fight came a woman of many cultures: African, Native American, and white. She would use her legacy and the wisdom it brought her to shake New Orleans and its citizens from their heads to their shoes. Her

name was Marie Laveau. In time, she became one of the most well-known and powerful Voodoo priestesses in the city. At the height of her fame, in the mid-1800s, she was known as the Voodoo Queen of New Orleans.

Her followers swore she could do magic. She was definitely a showman. She mixed Voodooism with Catholicism and made the religion more dramatic. But that also made it feel familiar to more people of New Orleans. People flocked to her in the hundreds. She made money selling spells and charms, like gris gris bags—tiny cloth bags filled with items that people thought had power: semi-precious stones, dried flowers, flower petals, spices, oils, and always a lock of the bag owner's hair.

These bags were tucked away in the owners' purses or pockets to bring them money, power, or luck.

When Marie Laveau was young, she worked as a hairdresser. She learned that women liked to talk while their hair was being styled. Women from every walk of life went to Marie, especially the rich and powerful. Marie chatted with these women as they boasted about bad things they'd done, lies they told, laws they'd broken, and items they had stolen. Marie kept a record of these secrets. Later, after she became a priestess, she kept collecting secrets of the wealthy and famous by talking to those who worked for them and knew them well. She would use these secrets against the rich and powerful, especially slave owners, who hurt and oppressed her followers.

Because Marie was so helpful and knowledgeable, her followers loved her.

Everyone else was terrified of her. For instance, a father came to Marie for help with his son who had been accused of several crimes. He told Marie that the real criminals were some friends of his son, who were making him take the blame. Marie agreed to help, and the father told her he would give her a house if his son was released.

Marie gathered three small peppers and hid them in her mouth. She spent the day infusing them with her intentions. Then she went to the courthouse. She laid the three peppers under the chair of the judge and then took a seat to watch the trial. The peppers were placed so no one but the judge could see them. She also made sure the judge would see her, the famous Voodoo Queen, in his courtroom for the trial. By the end of the case, despite the large amount of evidence against the boy, the judge's ruling was "not guilty." Was the judge afraid of the power of Voodoo that Marie was known to use? Or was he afraid of the secrets Marie knew? Either way, the father got his son back, and Marie got her house in an excellent part of town, where she lived out the rest of her life.

Marie is still the Voodoo Queen today, although she died in 1881. She is entombed somewhere in New Orleans. Because of her fame and power, at least five cemeteries claim to have her body within their gates. It is said her rowdy spirit could not be contained. People became afraid of her ghost and avoided the cemeteries. Cemetery owners make money showing off their cities of the dead to visitors to New Orleans, so they didn't want a ghost scaring them off. It is said that another Voodoo priestess helped move Marie to a secret place in an unnamed cemetery.

Wherever Marie is resting, the cemetery most people go to celebrate her is St. Louis Cemetery No. 1. Tourists and believers flock to the vault they hope holds her spirit and leave small gifts as offerings in the belief that they will have more luck in their lives with the blessing of the Voodoo Queen.

Of course, people swear they've seen Marie's ghost in the graveyard, walking the paths and visiting tombs. One man reports he got slapped by her after making an ugly comment about her resting place.

Another story people love to tell occurred in the 1930s. A homeless man chose to sleep in the cemetery one night. He climbed up on top of a tomb and fell into a deep sleep. In the middle of the night, he awoke to a strange noise. He worried that thieves had come to rob tombs of their statues and decorations. He decided sleeping on top of one of them wasn't the best idea after all. He climbed down from the tomb and headed for the front gate.

As he crept toward the exit, he came upon the tomb of Marie Laveau. The tomb seemed to glow with a hidden light, and a ghostly woman, with a large snake coiled around her body, was dancing wildly with a large group of other ghosts. These spirit men and women danced their savage celebration in complete silence. Terrified they would attack him, the homeless man ran as fast as he could to the exit.

Marie's followers claim that Marie rises once a year to lead them to prayer. The day, June 23, is also called St. John's Eve, a famous Voodoo and Christian holiday in New Orleans.

There are also rumors that she practices Voodoo in her old house. People say they have seen her and several ghosts of her supporters involved in ceremonies there. New Orleanians say you will know her by her famous blue tignon, a large cloth which is worn around the head and tied off with seven knots.

Marie has also apparently been seen in a house where she lived as a young woman. It is claimed that her ghost has been seen hovering by the fireplace.

Another favorite story comes again from the 1930s. A customer ordered some medication from a pharmacist. An elderly lady in pale clothes and a blue tignon walked up to stand beside the customer. The pharmacist's face distorted in terror, and he bolted into the back of his store.

The customer turned to look at the woman who caused such a reaction. The woman let out a crazy cackling laugh. The customer wondered why the pharmacist was scared of this strange lady who probably lived in the neighborhood. The woman stopped laughing and asked him if he knew who she was. The customer shook his head. The woman became angry, asked where the pharmacist had gone, and slapped the customer in his face. She then ran out of the store and disappeared over the wall of the cemetery across the street.

The customer fainted. The pharmacist came back and woke him by giving him a swig of whiskey. The customer asked who the woman was, and the pharmacist told him she was Marie Laveau, who had died years ago but still shows up every now and then. Then he told him he'd been slapped by the Voodoo Queen of New Orleans.

Royal Street, New Orleans

CHAPTER 4

Prove Your Love

Royal Street is the most famous street in the French Quarter of New Orleans. There you can find art galleries, antique shops, live music, and delicious food—plus a ghost! But it is said that you can only see this ghost on the coldest nights of December when even the sun-loving New Orleanians have to bundle up in coats and scarves and lots of warm clothing. Although rare, New Orleans has freezing weather at times.

The people who've seen the ghost say she wanders on the rooftop without a coat. She wears nothing warm to protect her at all. When the wind sweeps over her, she hunkers down, hugging herself with her arms in a losing attempt to stay warm. They say she can be seen all night, but if you go up to search for her, you will find nothing but the empty roof. But come the next freezing night, you can see her walking the roof again.

Her name was Julie, it is said, and she lived in the building where her ghost now walks. She was a sweet girl who fell in love with a wealthy and powerful man. The man loved her too, but the wealthy and powerful people of the past had strict ideas about who they could and couldn't be with. The rich and mighty must marry other wealthy or powerful people. Julie didn't have much of either of those things at all.

The man she loved explained all of this. He agreed to see Julie in secret but told her there would never be a wedding between the two of them. Julie was heartbroken. She argued, begged, and pleaded, hoping she could persuade the man she loved to throw aside his family's wishes and society's rules and marry her.

The young man refused, telling her it would never work. Too many would condemn the marriage and that would make both of them miserable. But Julie responded that she was already miserable. The two lovebirds began to grow apart.

The young man missed their relationship. Breaking up with Julie was not something he wanted to do. Even thinking about it was more than he could bear. So he came up with a plan.

He would tell her she needed to prove her love to him by completing the following task: when the clock struck midnight that night, she should go out onto the roof. She was not to wear a coat or any other warm clothing. She would then spend the rest of the night outside in the freezing weather. New Orleans, at that time, was having a spell of unusually icy weather; in fact, earlier in the day, it had been sleeting.

The young man was sure Julie would refuse such an impossible undertaking. He expected she would stare at him and then laugh at his demand. He hoped she would then realize that marriage between them was impossible, but they could still go on loving each other without having to upset his family and friends.

But Julie agreed to do the task.

The young man did not believe her and was

so sure she wouldn't go through with it, that he left to have drinks and play chess with a friend.

Julie prepared herself, then opened the door and stepped into the darkness. The young man spent the whole night out with his friend. He came back to the apartment, exhausted and content with the fun he'd had only to find Julie was not at home. He remembered the demand he had made of her and panicked. He truly never believed she would do such a dangerous thing. He raced up the stairs to the roof and found her, collapsed against a wall. Stunned and in agony, he ran to her lifeless body. He fought to awaken her, but she had already left this world.

Julie's old home still stands. She is said to still appear on the roof in December to walk the night away and then dwindle into nothing in the early light.

The folks who now live there say that the rooftop is not the only place Julie haunts. People in neighboring rooms hear footsteps in her old apartment. A phantom of a young man playing chess will drift in and out at times in the building—possibly Julie's young man, tormenting himself with her loss.

A tearoom has opened on the ground floor, and the staff reports tapping sounds and the scent of a heavenly perfume that overwhelms the air then fades away. Behind the tearoom, there is a pretty courtyard with trees, flowers, and goldfish splashing in a decorative pond. Julie's reflection appears to a few lucky patrons at times. And someone once caught sight of her as she turned a corner. Many feel Julie will never leave. She is tied by her love of her home and the man

to whom she gave everything. Now there is a moral to this story. If someone you love tells you that you must prove your love for them, don't. As Julie would tell you, it never turns out well.

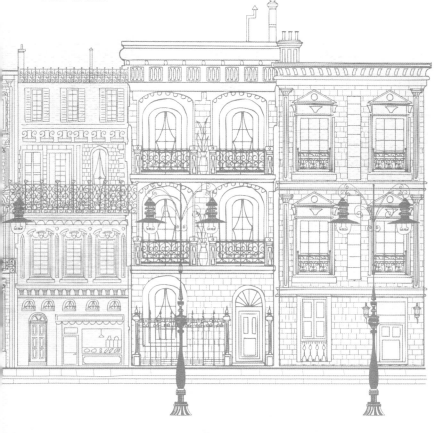

Beauregard-Keyes House

The Phantom Army

Visitors to the French Quarter in New Orleans have found the Beauregard-Keyes House, with its Civil War-era furniture and decorations, a fascinating look into the late 1800s. General Beauregard was a commander in the Confederate army. After he was defeated in the war, he came back to New Orleans and settled into the house to live out the rest of his life. After he died, the property passed through several other owners who made changes to the historic house.

Finally, a group of people who lived in the area grew concerned that the famous place would be ruined if that continued. Together, they bought the house and turned it into a historical museum dedicated to the Civil War and the general.

Soon after the museum opened, strange stories began to circulate in the neighborhood about the old house. People claimed to hear battle sounds coming from the building and the garden—sounds like cannon and musket fire and the screams of men. The neighbors called it the "Phantom Army," but the tour guides who work at the house deny that any such thing exists.

However the guides will admit there are other ghostly goings-on. A young woman who once rented the apartment below the ballroom complained one day that people had a party up in the ballroom and kept her awake all night by moving furniture and playing music. But she was informed that she was the only person in the house that night.

So who threw a party? It is said that General Beauregard and his wife once had to cancel a fabulous party at the last minute. So now sometimes the ghosts of the couple come back to host the wonderful ball.

There are two other ghosts that the tour guides know of. One is a cat that brushes past people. The staff calls her Caroline. The other ghost is Lucky, the spirit of a cocker spaniel owned by Francis Parkinson Keyes, a famous author who lived in the house for a while. After her owner passed away, Lucky died as well. People say the dog never left the house again.

For evidence that the dog is there, the guides tell the story of a blind woman who once visited the house with her seeing-eye dog. They toured the house, but when they reached the bedroom where Keyes and

Lucky slept, the guide dog became frightened. The blind woman remarked that there must be another dog in the room. The tour guide denied this, saying no dogs had lived there for many years. The blind woman insisted a dog was there, saying her dog only behaved that way was when she was in the presence of another. What do you think?

CHAPTER 6

Locked Up

Jails and prisons are scary places even *without* ghosts. But several jails in New Orleans are lucky enough to have cells haunted by people who once resided there. The Old Carrollton Jail is one of the most well-known.

In the 1800s, the jail was being run by Sergeant William Clifton. One day, a woman and two men came by to chat with Sergeant Clifton. The men began the conversation, and the woman walked over to a wall and casually leaned against it. Suddenly she was thrown out of the room by a force coming from the wall. She stumbled and fell flat in the next room. The men turned and laughed, thinking she had somehow slipped. The shocked and surprised woman yelled back that something in the wall shoved her.

This made the men laugh even more.

Annoyed, the woman got up and again leaned on the wall in the same place. This time she was thrown into the men. She repeated that there was something in the wall. Then each man, including Sergeant Clifton, took a turn leaning on the wall. Each man was shoved away. Thinking it was a prank of some sort, they examined the wall, but nothing out of the ordinary was discovered.

Sergeant Clifton then remembered an

event that happened before he worked there. A man who murdered his wife was arrested and brought to the jail. A fight started between him and the police officers who had arrested him. The man was killed. He died right at the spot where Sergeant Clifton and his guests had been thrown from the wall. Could this man's spirit be shoving people from the wall? Clifton told them he couldn't believe it even though he'd felt it himself. He was sure he could find a logical reason at some point.

A few days later, another strange thing happened. Sergeant Clifton owned a picture of General Beauregard that hung on his wall. Sergeant Clifton was a big fan of the general and enjoyed saluting the picture at times. A patrolman named Perez came into the office and commented on the portrait. They chatted about the general for a while, and then Clifton turned and saluted the picture. With a loud crash, the picture fell from the wall, and a nearby washstand seemed to spring forward and fall to the ground. The two men checked the nail and cord that held the picture to the wall. The nail remained solidly in place, and the cord was unbroken. The patrolman and the sergeant could

find no reason for the picture to have fallen.

The next night, Clifton and Perez were relating the mystery of the picture crashing to the ground to some fellow officers. While he was talking, Clifton showed them how he saluted the portrait. This time, the mirror below the picture flew from the wall, smashing into the washstand and knocking it over again. This time, the whole group investigated the nail holding the mirror, and once again, it was found solidly in place.

The next event was even more startling. Sergeant Clifton was working at his desk when he was grabbed by his shoulders and spun around in his chair. He leaped to his feet and ran out of the office, thinking one of his men was playing a prank on him, but no one was there.

The strange happenings continued. Clifton

had a big soft sofa his men liked to take naps on when they worked overtime. One night, Officer Dell took an unexpected ride on the couch. The minute he lay down, the sofa was yanked away from the wall by an unseen force. The couch slid three feet out and then threw itself back against the wall. This was the same wall where the sergeant and his friends had been pushed.

The next officer who tried to nap on the sofa got the same ride, but in his case, the sofa tilted forward and threw him completely off its cushions. He was hurled, yelling, into the edge of Clifton's desk. His head was cut open by the impact. Clifton heard the yelp and raced in only to watch the couch slide—by itself—back to the wall.

One of Clifton's men, when told of the incident, laughed and accused them of trying to fool him. He lay down on the couch with everyone watching and was instantly thrown to the floor. No one wanted to take naps on the couch anymore until someone thought to put it in another room. There, naps were taken in peace.

The officers of the Old Carrollton Jail would tell you that the wall ghost was not the only spirit in the jail. One night, Corporal Harry Hyatt, alone in the office, heard odd footsteps. It was the sound of someone dragging their foot while they walked. He searched everywhere but found no one. He did notice that the hallway outside of the office smelled like cigar smoke. Corporal Hyatt knew there was a man, Officer Foster, on guard at the front of the building. He hurried down to see if he'd let anyone in. Officer Foster said no. But when he heard about the sound of the dragging foot, he said maybe Harvey had paid a visit.

Harvey was once a prisoner in the jail. He was a huge man who had a bad leg and walked with a limp. He also liked cigars. Harvey, even though a giant, managed to sneak out of the jail after ambushing two guards. Corporal Hyatt laughed, saying since Harvey got away so completely, he'd never come back and risk being captured again.

On his way home after his shift, Corporal Hyatt bought a paper and saw a story about a huge man named Robert Brewer who walked with a limp and lived up north. The man had passed away, and it was discovered that his real name was Harvey and he was wanted in New Orleans for escaping from jail. Corporal Hyatt then believed Harvey indeed had come back for a visit, since he knew he couldn't be locked up again.

The next night, the limping footsteps were back. Corporal Hyatt listened as they shuffled up and down the hallway over and over. Finally, he said, "Okay Harvey, you can stop your pacing and smoke your cigar now." The invisible feet stopped, and a giant cloud of smoke floated down the hall toward him.

The strange incidents continued. Items were lifted up and thrown at officers or fell from desks. More pictures fell off walls. One officer walked into a room and saw a picture spinning on the wall. He ran down the hall calling for others to come see, but the picture had stopped by the time they got back to look.

Despite the ghostly activity, no one was seriously hurt until the early morning, when Sergeant Clifton got attacked by an invisible pair of hands. He was sitting alone at his desk when two strong hands gripped him around his throat. His air cut off, he began to struggle, throwing his arms up to strike and scratch at the face of the attacker behind him. His hands found nothing. They simply waved around in the empty air. The feeling of the hands on his neck disappeared though. He spun around and saw no one, but everyone in the jail could see the big black bruises the hands had left on his neck. The marks didn't fade until a week later.

Officers weren't the only victims of the ghosts in the Old Carrollton Jail. Not while prisoners were held in Cell No. 3.

A prisoner named Charles Marquez was locked in Cell No. 3 for the night. When morning came, the guards found Marquez lying on the floor. The guards had to carry him out of the cell because he couldn't walk. In fact, he could barely talk. And even though he had been in the cell by himself, his face was battered and had cuts all over it.

Sergeant Clifton asked the man if one of his officers had beaten him, but Marquez said no. He insisted he had been beaten by unknown, invisible attackers. After that, every prisoner placed in Cell No. 3 came out beaten up and cut, often blaming ghosts for their injuries. Prisoners in nearby cells swore they heard nothing the whole night. Finally, someone remembered that several years ago, three murderers were locked into Cell No. 3 together. They spent the night attacking one another

until the morning came. When officers checked on them, two of them had been killed, and the last one died before they could get help. Clifton and his men wondered if they were the problem with Cell No. 3.

In 1937, the Carrollton Jail was demolished. The men who helped tear the building down reported human forms made of dust, dancing as though happy about the destruction of the lockup.

New Orleans

Tourist Trappers

Visitors come to New Orleans for many reasons, including beautiful buildings on the old-fashioned streets of the French Quarter, quaint hotels, and delicious food. Of course, in a city as haunted as New Orleans, one would expect to find ghosts in those hotels and restaurants as well. Let's begin with the Andrew Jackson Hotel on Royal Street.

The Andrew Jackson hotel was in a very old, very interesting building. Way back when Spain ruled the city, the Andrew Jackson Hotel was a boy's boarding school. One night, a terrible fire swept through the school, killing five of the boys who lived there. After the tragedy, the school building sat empty for a long time.

Finally, the old school was sold, and the new owners turned it into the hotel. Shortly after the hotel opened, the owners began hearing complaints about how loud the children were.

Guests insisted that they could hear children playing all over the hotel and in the gardens. They spoke of screams of laughter, kids yelling to one another, and every now and then something that sounded like a scream of terror. Could someone please quiet them down?

The staff could only tell them there were no children at the hotel.

It is thought that the boys lost in the fire have never left the old school. They play there still, running around the place together, having lots of noisy fun.

On Chartres Street, the Hotel Provincial is another haunted hotel. A guest who stayed there told a friend that he saw the spirit of a Confederate soldier. He said that as long as you didn't mind a ghost or two, it was the best hotel in New Orleans.

Why would ghost soldiers be at the hotel? The building that is now the Hotel Provincial was once a hospital called the Royal Military Hospital. Confederate soldiers wounded in battle were sent there. From time to time, employees of the hotel—as well as the guests—report running into misty men on crutches and ghost doctors in the hotel and on the grounds. The housekeepers report finding bloodstains on the sheets of the beds they are about to make, only to turn around again and see that the stains are gone.

Visitors have heard groaning and voices where no people are. Doors open and close with no hands pushing them. Weird cold spots appear in one place only to be felt again in another place later in the day. A haunted hotel indeed.

Next stop is Orleans Street and the Bourbon Orleans Hotel. In addition to the usual lights and TVs blinking on and off in different rooms, the faucets in this hotel turn themselves on in the night.

There is a ghost of a young woman who stays at the window of the Gabrielle Room. She appears to spend much of her eternal time watching people in the pool area. A ghost of a

Confederate soldier often wanders around in the front of the ballroom. A guest was shaken to his core when a depressed-seeming man walked right through him as he entered one of the men's bathrooms. There are voices of children crying or laughing in areas where no children are staying.

Once, an attendant was setting up for a big party when she noticed that the glassware she had carefully laid out on the table had been moved. She believed the ghost children were to blame because of the giggles of unseen children she heard right before the glassware shifted.

A cook setting up for a large party dropped a pair of pans he intended to use. Feeling like a fool, he cursed himself loudly. Instantly the lights went out, and someone slapped him across the face. The lights flickered back on, and no one was there. The cook ran to a mirror and saw a red hand mark on his face. He quit his job that very day.

And then there is Raul. A playful ghost who seems to enjoy appearing next to women, giving them a brilliant smile, and then fading away. Women who stay at the hotel seem to enjoy Raul's lighthearted greeting.

As for restaurants, many of them serve up more than heavenly food. O'Flaherty's was an Irish Pub on Toulouse Street that had three ghosts: the husband and wife who once lived there, Joseph and Mary Baptandier, and an unknown young woman who was murdered by Joseph right before he ended his own life.

Mary is most often seen by diners arriving for dinner as she peers out of a second-story

window. Her husband is encountered wandering about in the courtyard.

But the most popular ghost is the young woman Joseph did away with. She is known by her long brown hair and seems to like staying in the garden area. People know she's around when men or children feel an invisible hand sliding into their hands or playing around with their hair.

Commander's Palace on Washington Avenue is said to be haunted by the alcohol-loving original owner of the place, Emile Commander. He opened the restaurant back in 1880. The story goes that people first realized Emile's ghost was around when a waiter filled several glasses of wine ahead of a dinner party in a closed room. When the diners got to the table, one glass had been emptied.

No one else had been in the room.

After that, staff members would find dishes and silverware shifted from where they'd put them. Sometimes they would be found in a completely different room. And wine and other alcoholic beverages continued to disappear from the glasses they were poured into. No doubt the work of Emile.

The Old Absinthe House on Bourbon Street is home to several ghosts: an unknown woman, a wandering child, and group of ghostly partiers. But there is one who is a bit of a celebrity: the pirate Jean Lafitte. Way back during the American Revolution Lafitte worked with Andrew Jackson to save New Orleans from the British. The two men would sit for hours in the Old Absinthe House, drawing up their plans for what became the Battle of New Orleans.

In current days, Lafitte's ghost has been seen in full dress regalia in different places in the building. A staffer was changing his clothes in front of a mirror one day. He glanced

into the mirror and saw a man staring back at him wearing a hat, an unbuttoned shirt, and a bright scarlet sash around his waist. The staffer turned, ready to yell at the uninvited guest, and found no one there.

Lafitte was also seen in the liquor room. A staffer noticed the old-time costume the man on the stairs wore: an unbuttoned shirt and deep-blue pants. When Lafitte realized he had been seen, he approached the staffer, grinning at her and then walked right through the heavy wooden bar and vanished.

As you can see, New Orleans embraces her ghosts no matter how heartbreaking, wicked, or terrifying they may be. There are even ghost tours that visit some of the spots that ghosts are rumored to haunt. If you ever visit, rest assured that the living and the dead will welcome your stay. *Laissez les bon ton rouler!* Let the good times roll!

Laura Roach Dragon grew up in the magical city of New Orleans amidst parades, food fests, and hurricanes. She is a social worker and has written two middle grade books, *Hurricane Boy*, which won the Crystal Kite award, and *The Bayou Bogeyman Presents Voodoo and Hoodoo*, an anthology of scary stories.

Check out some of the other Spooky America titles available now!

Spooky America was adapted from the creeptastic Haunted America series, for adults. Haunted America explores historical haunts in cities and regions across America. Each book chronicles both the widely known and less-familiar history behind local ghosts and other unexplained mysteries. Here's more from the original *Haunted New Orleans* author Troy Taylor:

www.americanhauntingsink.com